THE CANDOUR OF A TESTAMENT

By

CLEMENT O. FASHORO

TABLE OF CONTENTS

A TWIST OF LIBERTY...

When the shifting
Sands of life
Goes out...
The point of retreat
Becomes
A shibboleth...

Like a shetland pony
In a hazy dusk
We run...
Past the
Howling shenanigans

In the shroud
Of gloomy secrecy
We courageously
Put down the shutters
On sidling
The whisper
At night
We get across
The rubicon...

From truth
And revelation
We find
The redemption
From hunger
And starvation
We milk...
Some consolation

Though ...
Our wings
Are clipped
Our aptitudes
Live in liberty...
Afflicted with
Utmost wretchedness
We joyously
Live in clover

From close quarters
Of
Danger zones
We had
A close shave
Of our lives...
In distress
And patent animosity
We clad ourselves
With harmony.

PRAISE ME NOT!!!

Praise me and saddle me
with burden.
Mock me and relieve me
of a burden.
Because praises
are never genuine prizes,
But acknowledgement
resultant from sentiments.

Praises are always shower
out of nought,
Therefore be mindful
of such praises,
Which portray you
as the best fruit of mankind,
And later prove
to be mockery.

An honest critic

is the sincerest friend,

But not so with

the sincerest praiser.

For each one has

different objective.

The former

is to tame

While the latter

is to maim.

It has always been

from time to time

That through undue praises

Many have become ruined

They fly high

in hopeless ego,

And later crashed

into oblivion.

CLEMENT O. FASHORO

SAVE THE AFRICAN CHILDREN

Give me a chance

And I shall grow

To puberty and adulthood

I can grow

Give me a chance.

I have the wish to grow

I should grow

With efforts and determination

I will grow

Give me a chance.

I have the ambition to grow
I have to grow
Without embargo, with free
hands
I must grow
Give me a chance.

I have growth potential
I want to grow
In free and peaceful
atmosphere
I will grow
Give me a chance.

AND THE WINTER CAME...

And the winter came
At the heartbeat of summer
With a thong to the tonsils
That comes with throngs of decisions

Decisions born of despair
And desire
And dreary tears to weep

A cold ash burrowed
Into the hourglass
A frosty gong
Knelling us to our yesterdays

A whimper that prowls

Our nights

With the bleeding bruise

We sidle to the dawn

The Winter bites

Are not the freezing point

Neither the frosted moments

But our heart rendering

That squeezes tears

Out of our pitiful soul

Tinkering our actions

Back to the syllables

Of our punctured ego

Leading to denouement

Kissing the dust.

CLEMENT O. FASHORO

THE RESONANCE OF END...

Death is not an achive

Laid out to the beyond,

A tooting enigma,

Every breathing day

We visit its museum

By our pulsating lungs

That dance in heave

In and out

Of its threshold

And we say what is life?

When death is always

A grin away

Batting at us

In garish colours,

Our clock simpers

At us to the willows

That eventually render us inane.

We are here

Playing moronic

With the tutorials

Of the unending silence

We thrive to cage

The peace beneath

The prisms of sunken wood of dreams

We borrow few drops

Of liquid glasses

Into our terracotta

Eyeballs

Flooding our faces

Down the streamline

Of our sorry cheeks

Mirroring our nothingness

At the sight of a grave

A lesson we whisker

Until our utmost is grounded

To a shattering halt

A whimper we 'rite'

Flailing as sorrow

But,

There's a calm

Beneath

A more restful harbour,

Beneath

The green fields,

A stark quietude

Beneath,

Beneath the soul of a pauper

And vastness of the affluent,

And it's coming

It is here

It is our companion

It's the stark nude simper

At the end of our misstep

Where all egos

Are smothered

In equal furnace

And we cool off inane

At the howling end of night

The night of all nights.

CONFINED...

I am locked up
In the walls
Of my bowel self

I watch my words
Crawling up my cranny
Building towers

Against the vices
Of my doubts
Sprawling in my soul

The liberty
Of my very eyes
Has betrayed me

Just one look
At my heart
With a little padlock...

I am rowdy inside
Subtly lethal outside
Nigh oblivious...

Remorse has built
Upon the bricks
Of my saddled guilt

Can you aid me out?
Can you let out
My words averred?

Unbroken apart?
With truth avowed?
And bully detained?

Speechless noon rise
Bellow aloft
To a standstill...

I guess the world
Has aired my plight
Untamed can I express?

27

Pen and Parchment

Oh, Heart With Blithe!
Give me them

And let me rewrite

Your lore in beatitude...

For I am smitten

By the quills...

The parchment,

My ledger of testaments

Upon every drop

Of ink...

I can redirect your

Trajectories

I can seek you

Out of inane boredom

I can twinkle your passion
To stupor
I can beat your sorrow
To pulp

I will widen your horizon
You will taste
The brine
Of grand imaginings...

All I ask is
A peek of your eyes,
A whiff of your ears,
A fleck of your heart...

For your groping eyes,
They will clasp
To stash away
At immortality of loving

Your whispering ears,
They shall hone
To embrace
The odes of paradise

And your gleeful heart
Shall race faster
Than a galloping horse
Towards exquisiteness...

May I adorably sit
My thawing hands
Into your frosted essence
Where my tongue
Has failed to splinter.

My Astute Motives...

I whisper love
To blot out the stains
In your cherished memories

I trade away sorrow
For kindness to give
Meanings to living

I forge some silence
For hearts to listen
To the quiet rhythms
They always play

I loosen the strings of hope
For faith to have
Its proper feet
Duck in belief

I flag up doubts
In all aces of trust
For reasons to hold reigns

I elude my discovery
Watching...
How each one falters
Upon my thoughts

I paint some measure
Of distance
To know who can see
Past my portrait

Hidden within blushed eyes
I see many spirits
Baying for freedom

I entreat minds
To shun off robes
That fasten many souls
To distraught needs

I lay firm trust
In many stitched lies and
deceits
Of some people
In search of wisdom

I have observed
How small a weight
Can bear
Much heavy burdens

I am moulding
The clay of my wounds
Into something
Of cherished worth...

I am giving your wits
Some embers...
Igniting your spirit
Just to see your meteor spark

The Very Astute Of My Life...

WE MUST BE KINDLED

From the ocean of gloom, spread the gilded
sunshine in your vase around.

That's the only tentacles that blanket away sorrow.

Till we find laughter, our bathing suit, let's sweeten
the cords of sour memories that lead to our trepid
now.

Even if the cold in its extremism has decreed a let
up, and the winter has lost its chanterelle, expunged
the fragrances of cloves,

The docile sun in our hearts can still afford the rambling warmth, spread across its strengthening summer.

No hope is forever forlorn, if the heart remains un-stale.

Promises unmade can still be fulfilled by the vigor of The Unknown.

41

Dear Melancholia,

What a sprinting killjoy you humbly are! A rancour
in the heart of sweetness.

A dreary, taciturn simper in the face of desire.

You're a stiff breeze, clanging against all chains of
goodness.

Delousing one's soul against such a slamming snow
bar...

Is a wheel that has to take a thousand torques,
orbiting itself against the fiery embers.

It's like arthritis biting off your age at the sight of
happiness.

The FOUR Letters Of EVE...

The Four letters of EVEnings...
Of its darkness
Of its sleep
Of its dreams...
Is but a WISH.

The Four letters of EVEryone...
To her yearnings
To her intents
To her chance...
Is LUCK.

The Four letters of all EVEnts...
For their painfuls
For their glamours
For their timelines...
Is DATE.

The Four letters of EVErything...
Of its puzzles
Of its growlings
Of its summations...
Is LIFE.

The four letters of EVEn...
From its equators
From its swings
From its balance...
Is JUST.

The Fours letters of EVErest...
Of its impregnations
Of its indignations
Of its inclinations...
Is MIND.

The Four letters of EVErgreen...
By its precious
By its freshness
By its unendings...
Is TIME.

The Four letters of EVErmore...
In its suspense
In its passion
In its beatitude...
Is the CARE.

The Four letters of EVErywhere...
Through its cravings
Through its mazes
Through its doors...
Is but a CLUE.

The Four letters of EVErlasting...

Making it immortal

Making it unwavering

Making it believable...

Is to be TRUE.

The Four letters of EVE...

From the soul

...of her tears

From the fears

...of her cares

From the sheer
...of her breaths

From the years
...of her snares

Of her kiss
...to her seeds

Of her tease
...to her ease

Of her needs
...to her deeds

... Is LOVE.

9 798846 413436